DREAM HORSES
A Poster Book

Text by Deborah Burns
Photographs by Bob Langrish
Artwork by Elsebeth Christensen

Dream Horses

Throughout history, horses have ambled, loped, and cantered through our dreams. It's not surprising: For thousands of years we've been partners with these majestic animals in work, play, and sport. Long ago, horses carried knights in battle, plowed fields, raced before kings, rounded up cattle, and helped settlers spread through the Americas. More recently they hauled the wagons that delivered our grandparents' morning milk, pulled streetcars and fire trucks through city streets, and carried pupils across the prairies to one-room schoolhouses. Until well into the twentieth century, they were a vital part of our lives and we depended on them every day. (Once there were as many types of horse-drawn carts and carriages as today there are types of cars and trucks!)

Many cultures have loved, studied, and honored horses, from early Arab, Mongol, and Native American breeders to military horsemen, from Spanish and Mexican vaqueros to English royalty. Over the ages, horses have swept into the legends and lore of different lands as symbols of beauty, purity, spirit, fire, and freedom. Because horses and humans fit together so well, they were thought to be the gifts of God. In many different myths they carried riders between spirit worlds. The Bedouins thought they drank the wind; the Greeks thought they drew the sun. The Native Americans considered them spirits that made humans complete.

Let's meet some of the dream horses that make our lives complete.

"*And the breed of horses they reared could not be surpassed in the world—
they were made of fire and flame, and not of dull, heavy earth.*"

— ENCYCLOPEDIA OF THE FAIRIES

"His mane is like a river flowing,
And his eyes like embers glowing
In the darkness of the night,
And his pace as swift as light."
— BRYAN WALLER PROCTOR, *THE BLOOD HORSE*

"He was a giant of a horse, glistening black. The head was that of the wildest of all wild creatures —and it was beautiful, savage, splendid. A stallion with a wonderful physical perfection that matched his savage, ruthless spirit."

—WALTER FARLEY, *THE BLACK STALLION*

"On the wings of the morning they gather and fly,
In the hush of the night time I hear them go by,
The horses of memory thundering through
With flashing white fetlocks all wet with the dew."

—WILL H. OGILVIE, *THE HOOVES OF HORSES*

"The air of heaven is that which blows between a horse's ears."
—ARABIAN PROVERB

"He is pure air and fire; and the dull elements of earth and water never appear in him."

—WILLIAM SHAKESPEARE, *HENRY V*

"Gypsy gold does not clink and glitter. It gleams in the sun and neighs in the dark."
—GYPSY SAYING, COUNTY GALWAY, IRELAND

"He trots the air. The earth sings when he touches it."
—WILLIAM SHAKESPEARE, *HENRY V*

The mission of Storey Publishing is to serve our customers by publishing practical information that encourages personal independence in harmony with the environment.

Edited by Deborah Burns
Art direction by Lisa Clark
Design and production by Kathy Herlihy-Paoli

Photographs by Bob Langrish
Artwork by Elsebeth Christensen
Title page background image © Sabine Vollmer von Falken

Storey books are available for special premium and promotional uses and for customized editions. For further information, please call 1-800-793-9396.

Printed in China by Elegance
10 9 8 7 6 5 4 3 2

Library of Congress Cataloging-in-Publication Data

Burns, Deborah.
Dream horses poster book / Deborah Burns.
p. cm.
ISBN 1-58017-574-0 (pbk. : alk. paper)
1. Horses—Juvenile literature. 2. Horses—Pictorial works—Juvenile literature. I. Title.
SF302.H5 2004
636.1'0022'2—dc22
2004005582